# Formula 1 ™

Published by Ladybird Books Ltd 2009
A Penguin Company
Penguin Books Ltd, 80 Strand, London, WC2R 0RL, UK
Penguin Books Australia Ltd, Camberwell, Victoria, Australia
Penguin Books (NZ), 67 Apollo Drive, Rosedale, North Shore
0632, New Zealand (a divison of Pearson New Zealand Ltd)
www.ladybird.com

F1, FORMULA 1, FORMULA ONE, FIA FORMULA ONE WORLD
CHAMPIONSHIP, GRAND PRIX and related logos are trademarks
of Formula One Licensing BV. All rights reserved.

Written by Adam Hay-Nicholls

Photography credits:
© Martin Trenkler
With thanks to Renault, Williams, Bridgestone, Force India, Red
Bull Racing, BMW Sauber, Toro Rosso, Toyota, Brawn GP.

ISBN: 9781409303091
2
Printed in Great Britain

# Formula 1™

# FUEL-INJECTED
# FACT BOOK

Adam Hay-Nicholls

# CONTENTS

# INTRODUCTION

As I've travelled the world with the Formula One™ circus, reporting for newspapers and magazines, my thoughts have often strayed from the lap-time information screens and the action in the pits to wonder, if Ferrari were a rock band, who would they be? And which driver has the most pets?

By reading this book you will learn the answers to these questions and many more. Such as, which driver was also a champion budgerigar breeder? Do any of the drivers have embarrassing nicknames? What was the greatest overtaking move ever? Are drivers scared of anything? Have you got what it takes to get into F1™ racing? And, if you do, what should you do when you climb the steps of the podium?

This book is stuffed with interesting and often bizarre facts, stats and quizzes to test and enhance your knowledge and enjoyment of this exciting sport.

**Adam Hay-Nicholls**

# THE DRIVERS

**Welcome to the Class of 2009.** We all know these guys can drive, but who can play the piano, and who is the best at bowling? Match the drivers on pages 8-11 to the trivia on pages 12-15. You'll find the answers at the back of the book on page 96.

### Lewis Hamilton
Nationality: British
Date of birth: 7th January 1985
Team: McLaren

### Heikki Kovalainen
Nationality: Finnish
Date of birth: 19th October 1981
Team: McLaren

### Felipe Massa
Nationality: Brazilian
Date of birth: 25th April 1981
Team: Ferrari

### Kimi Räikkönen
Nationality: Finnish
Date of birth: 17th October 1979
Team: Ferrari

### Robert Kubica

**Nationality:** Polish
**Date of birth:** 7th December 1984
**Team:** BMW Sauber

### Nick Heidfeld

**Nationality:** German
**Date of birth:** 10th May 1977
**Team:** BMW Sauber

### Fernando Alonso

**Nationality:** Spanish
**Date of birth:** 29th July 1981
**Team:** Renault

### Nelson Piquet Jr

**Nationality:** Brazilian
**Date of birth:** 25th July 1985
**Team:** Renault

### Sebastian Vettel

**Nationality:** German
**Date of birth:** 3rd July 1987
**Team:** Red Bull Racing

### Mark Webber

**Nationality:** Australian
**Date of birth:** 27th August 1976
**Team:** Red Bull Racing

### Jarno Trulli

Nationality: Italian
Date of birth: 13th July 1974
Team: Toyota

### Timo Glock

Nationality: German
Date of birth: 18th March 1982
Team: Toyota

### Nico Rosberg

Nationality: German
Date of birth: 27th June 1985
Team: Williams

### Kazuki Nakajima

Nationality: Japanese
Date of birth: 11th January 1985
Team: Williams

### Rubens Barrichello

Nationality: Brazilian
Date of birth: 23rd May 1972
Team: Brawn GP

### Jenson Button

Nationality: British
Date of birth: 19th January 1980
Team: Brawn GP

## Sébastien Bourdais

**Nationality:** French
**Date of birth:** 28th February 1979
**Team:** Scuderia Toro Rosso

## Sébastien Buemi

**Nationality:** Swiss
**Date of birth:** 31st October 1988
**Team:** Scuderia Toro Rosso

## Giancarlo Fisichella

**Nationality:** Italian
**Date of birth:** 14th January 1973
**Team:** Force India

## Adrian Sutil

**Nationality:** German
**Date of birth:** 11th January 1983
**Team:** Force India

# DRIVER TRIVIA

How well do you know the F1™ drivers? Fancy yourself a bit of an expert? Take this quiz to find out.

**1** Because of his long blond hair, his mechanics have nicknamed him 'Britney'.

**2** **His father is a famous conductor and, until he switched his attention to go-karts, this driver was groomed as a concert pianist.**

**3** He's a talented tenpin bowler and competes in European championships when he's not racing.

**4** **This race winning driver is into camping, and likes to travel the French and Italian countryside in his gold 1960s Volkswagen camper van.**

**5** He's not from the West but he does like Westerns. The person he would most like to shake hands with is legendary actor and director Clint Eastwood.

**6** **Before he made it to F1 racing, this German gentleman earned money working as a scaffolder.**

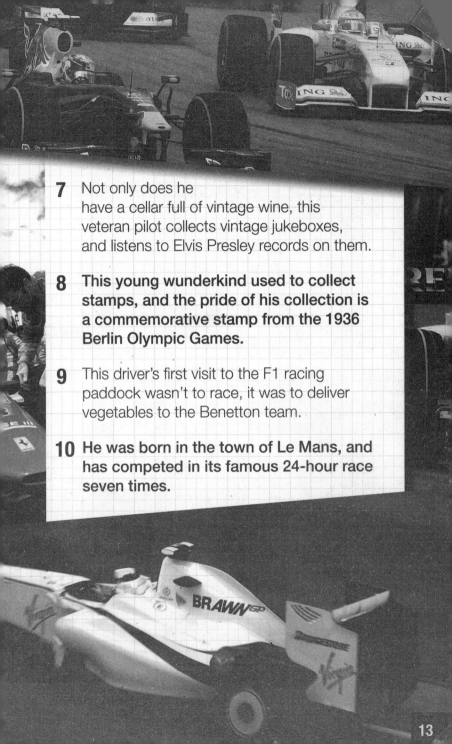

**7** Not only does he have a cellar full of vintage wine, this veteran pilot collects vintage jukeboxes, and listens to Elvis Presley records on them.

**8** This young wunderkind used to collect stamps, and the pride of his collection is a commemorative stamp from the 1936 Berlin Olympic Games.

**9** This driver's first visit to the F1 racing paddock wasn't to race, it was to deliver vegetables to the Benetton team.

**10** He was born in the town of Le Mans, and has competed in its famous 24-hour race seven times.

**11** This Finn can play the drums and was in a band at school.

**12** It may seem strange, but this world champion says he finds supermarket shopping a great way to relax. He loves the frozen-food aisle.

**13** This rookie drove the FIA medical car at the final three races of 2008.

**14** His yacht is named 'Fizzy'.

**15** Has driven in the more F1 than any other in the current line-up.

**16** His first car was a far cry from the Ferrari he drives today. It was a Lada.

**17** This gourmet driver's favourite food is foie gras,

a rich pâté made from fattened goose or duck liver.

**18** This animal lover from Down Under has two rescue donkeys, Ned and Oliver, a cat called Jet, a dog named Shadow and some goldfish too.

**19** If he wins three world championships, his boss has promised to give him his dream road car: The McLaren F1 LM – it's orange and worth over £1 million.

**20** He has a small scar on his cheek from being attacked by a dog when he was a child.

# WHOSE LID IS IT ANYWAY?

Do you know which helmet belongs to each driver?

Write the correct owner's name below each helmet, and turn to the back of the book to see if you're correct.

I

...............................

J

...............................

K

...............................

L

...............................

M

...............................

N

...............................

O

...............................

P

...............................

Q

...............................

R

...............................

S

...............................

T

...............................

# ROCK ON!

Being a Formula One™ driver is a bit like being a rock star. You've got the race engineer on guitar, software technicians on keyboards, the team spokesperson on backing vocals and the mechanics on the rhythm section.
So which band would each team be?

## McLaren
**Founded:** 1963
**Engine:** Mercedes-Benz   **Location:** Woking, UK
**Race drivers:** Lewis Hamilton, Heikki Kovalainen
**Team principal:** Martin Whitmarsh

**If McLaren were a band they would be:** Daft Punk
*This electronic band's distinctive suits and helmets are inspired by outer space. McLaren Mercedes sought similar inspiration when they built their factory and designed their team clothing. Their pit crew helmets are particularly 'Daft Punk', and they supplied composites for the Beagle 2 space probe.*

## Ferrari
**Founded:** 1947
**Engine:** Ferrari   **Location:** Maranello, Italy
**Race drivers:** Felipe Massa, Kimi Räikkönen
**Team principal:** Stefano Domenicali

**If Ferrari were a band they would be:** U2
*Fabulously successful, rich, highly political and have the ear of governments. Often popular with those who aren't so interested in the genre, but can nonetheless put on a flamboyant live show. Ferrari have a bit of a following too.*

# BMW Sauber

**Founded:** 1993 (as Sauber)
**Engine:** BMW   **Location:** Hinwil, Switzerland
**Race drivers:** Robert Kubica, Nick Heidfeld
**Team principal:** Dr Mario Theissen

**If BMW Sauber were a band they would be:** The Black Eyed Peas
*This band had plenty of credibility but little success until
they hired blond bombshell Fergie to provide vocals.
The record company shovelled in cash, and the group
became a global sensation. Since BMW took over
Sauber and hired blonde bombshell Nick Heidfeld,
they've started to do pretty well too.*

# Renault

**Founded:** 2002
**Engine:** Renault   **Location:** Enstone, UK
**Race drivers:** Fernando Alonso, Nelson Piquet Jr
**Team principal:** Flavio Briatore

**If Renault were a band they would be:**
The Strokes
*You just don't know what to expect from them.
They release one critically acclaimed album and
follow it up with a howler. Then, a couple of years
later, they're back on top and picking up awards. Renault, and its
former incarnation Benetton, has always blown hot and cold too.*

# Williams

**Founded:** 1977
**Engine:** Toyota   **Location:** Grove, UK
**Race drivers:** Nico Rosberg, Kazuki Nakajima
**Team principal:** Sir Frank Williams

**If Williams were a band they would be:** Radiohead
*These public school boys were huge until the late 90s and then went
experimental. Many thought they were done for when they separated
from their record company, but going independent suits them.
Williams won 16 world titles and designed a car with walrus tusks on
the front. Now they are the last of the true 'independents'.*

## Red Bull Racing

**Founded:** 2005
**Location:** Milton Keynes, UK
**Engine:** Renault
**Race drivers:** Sebastian Vettel,
Mark Webber
**Team principal:** Christian Horner

**If Red Bull Racing were a band they would be:** New Order
*Both were born out of an older outfit – New Order was formerly Joy Division, and RBR was previously Jaguar Racing. New Order has their own nightclub, the Hacienda, and Red Bull take their 'Energy Station' (complete with DJs) to every race in the calendar.*

## Toyota

**Founded:** 2002
**Location:** Cologne, Germany     **Engine:** Toyota
**Race drivers:** Jarno Trulli, Timo Glock
**Team Principal:** Tadashi Yamashina

**If Toyota were a band they would be:** Guns N' Roses
*It cost $13 million and fourteen years of recording time, but Guns N' Roses' 'Chinese Democracy' album only debuted at number two in the UK album chart. Toyota have the biggest budget of any team, but still the best they have to show for it is second place.*

## Scuderia Toro Rosso

**Founded:** 2006
**Location:** Faenza, Italy    **Engine:** Ferrari
**Race drivers:** Sébastien Bourdais,
Sébastien Buemi
**Team principal:** Franz Tost

**If Toro Rosso were a band they would be:**
The White Stripes
*This pared-back band only has two members, while the Toro Rosso team doesn't have its own design department, using that of sister team Red Bull Racing instead.*

# Brawn GP

**Founded:** 1999 (as British American Racing)
**Location:** Brackley, UK    **Engine:** Mercedes
**Race drivers:** Jenson Button, Rubens Barichello
**Team principal:** Ross Brawn

**If the team formerly known as Honda were a band they would be:** Oasis
*Oasis split with their record company to form their own, while Honda pulled the plug on F1 racing and left the Brackley-based team to fend for itself. The Gallagher brothers can never agree who the front man is. Chief Executive Nick Fry and Team Principal Ross Brawn may have a similar argument.*

# Force India

**Founded:** 2008
**Location:** Silverstone, UK    **Engine:** Mercedes
**Race drivers:** Giancarlo Fisichella, Adrian Sutil
**Team principal:** Dr Vijay Mallya

**If Force India were a band they would be:** Diddy
*The hip hop guy was christened Sean Combs, but changed his name to Puff Daddy. Then he was P. Diddy, and these days he just goes by Diddy. Meanwhile, the old Jordan team became Midland MF1, then Spyker, and now Force India. Team chief Vijay Mallya never leaves the house without diamond earrings. Not unlike Diddy.*

# LOGO LOWDOWN

Here are some logos, each from a current F1™ racing team. Well, actually they are only bits of logos.
**Can you correctly identify all ten teams?**

**A**

**B**

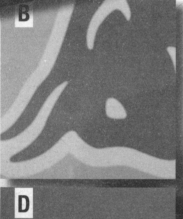

**C**

**D**

**E**

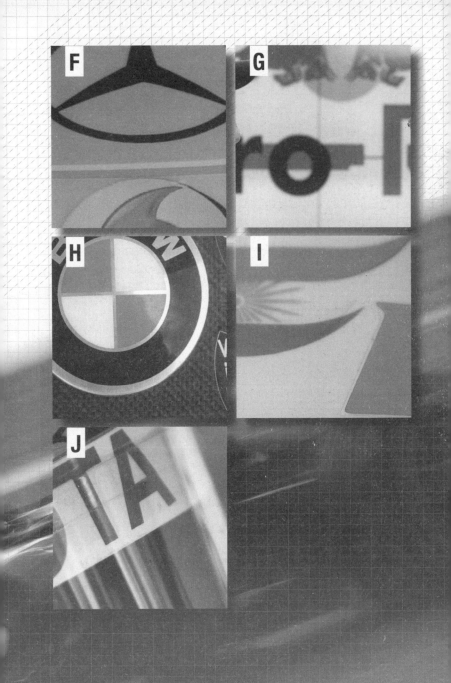

# KEEPING TRACK

F1™ drivers must be frequent victims of burglary, because everyone knows when they're out. Here's where they go between March and November, the low-down on all the circuits, and who you might meet there.

## Australian Grand Prix

*Melbourne*

**Celebrity guest:** Pint-sized Aussie pop sensation Kylie Minogue

This colourful circuit is set within beautiful parkland, but you can still see the skyscrapers of downtown Melbourne in the distance. The track usually produces a strong race, and often some spectacular crashes due to ever-present concrete walls. Safety car periods are frequent.

## Malaysian Grand Prix

*Kuala Lumpur*

Built on land that was formerly jungle, this circuit features a spectacular double-fronted grandstand for spectators and two super long straights. The track exposes drivers to incredibly hot and humid conditions, which makes the Sepang Circuit's demanding curves an even greater challenge.

**Celebrity guest:** Martial arts actor and director Jackie Chan

# Chinese Grand Prix
*Shanghai*

Its main grandstand – with suites built actually over the start-finish straight itself – dwarfs that of any other circuit. A tricky track on which to drive, it's quite punishing on tyres. A long back straight allows cars to draft each other and pass.

**Celebrity guest:**
Actor Keanu Reeves

# Bahrain Grand Prix
*Sakhir*

A special tarmac has been used on this track, so that grip will remain even when sand is blown across it. It is in a desert, after all, and sand can be an almighty problem for tyres and also engines. The drivers wear heavily-tinted visors, so they're not blinded by the sun that reflects off the dunes.

**Celebrity guest:**
British jazz-pop singer Jamie Cullum

# Spanish Grand Prix
*Catalunya*

So much pre-season testing is carried out at this track that it's said the drivers could steer around it blindfolded. And, because they're used to it, rarely does anyone make a mistake here, making overtaking difficult. While the 125,000 Fernando Alonso fans add some atmosphere, the first person through the first corner is usually favourite to win.

**Celebrity guest:**
Actor Owen Wilson

## Monaco Grand Prix
### *Monte Carlo*

Monaco is as much about the glamorous parties and famous guests as the race itself. It's incredibly tight and twisty, with no room for error. Cars shoot past yachts bobbing in the harbour, around cafes and through a tunnel. It's the race every driver wants to win more than any other. Make sure the winner buys the drinks – a cola costs up to £50!

**Celebrity guest:** Socialite Paris Hilton

## Turkish Grand Prix
### *Istanbul*

This modern circuit combines some of the best corners of other tracks. The first corner, for instance, was inspired by the 'Senna S' curve at Brazil's Interlagos track. The corner everyone gets excited about, though, is Turn Eight, a ferociously fast, flat-out double-apex left-hander which, like burnt sausages, is guaranteed to put hairs on your chest!

**Celebrity guest:** Retired American boxer Mike Tyson

## British Grand Prix
### *Silverstone*

Silverstone's mix of flowing corners and lengthy straights makes this a great test for both driver and car. The inclement British weather also makes it unpredictable. The home Grand Prix for the majority of teams, Silverstone hosted the first ever world championship Grand Prix in 1950. Previously, it was a wartime air base.

**Celebrity guest:** The Beckhams

# German Grand Prix
### *Nürburgring*

**Celebrity guest:** Film director and producer Quentin Tarantino

Built right next door to the widow-making 14-mile long Nürburgring Nordschleife, arguably the greatest racetrack ever conceived, the new Nürburgring, which started hosting Grands Prix in 1984, is a shadow of its former self. The old circuit was deemed too dangerous. Nonetheless, the new circuit does have some decent corners.

# Hungarian Grand Prix
## *Budapest*

The Hungaroring is often compared to a go-kart track, with its tight corners and minimal straights. In fact, it's a bit like Monaco, but without the buildings. As a result, overtaking is an irregular occurrence but nonetheless, this circuit has hosted some very memorable races.

**Celebrity guest:** Former fashion model Jodie Kidd

# European Grand Prix
## *Valencia*

**Celebrity guest:** Rock band Hard-Fi

Twenty-five corners – some tight chicanes and hairpins and sweeping high-speed bends – pack out this dockside street circuit. It even includes a distinctive swing bridge where F1 cars can fire across Valencia's waterway, after the super yachts have passed through and taken position.

# Belgian Grand Prix
## Spa-Francorchamps

**Celebrity guest:** Former No. 1 tennis champion Boris Becker

This is the greatest test of driver bravery. The plunge down from the La Source hairpin, up to the blind Eau Rouge crest – without lifting – is the stuff of legend. The weather can change minute-to-minute. The long straights and top gear turns make this a true power circuit.

# Italian Grand Prix
## Monza

Monza has changed somewhat since it held its first Grand Prix on its banking in 1922, but the spirit remains. Set in royal parkland, this circuit features endless straights, which allow the cars to run at well over 300km/h. The cars race with low downforce wing settings to allow minimum drag, making it harder to take corners but possible to achieve such eye-watering top speeds.

**Celebrity guest:** Professional footballer Ronaldo

# Singapore Grand Prix
## Singapore

**Celebrity guest:** Indian actress and model Shilpa Shetty

Formula One racing's only night race takes place in Singapore's Marina Bay area. Teams stay up all night working on their cars, sleep until the afternoon and then go racing at dinner time. There are so many floodlights along the course, though, so to the drivers it seems like daylight.

## Japanese Grand Prix
*Suzuka*

**Celebrity guest:** Supermodel Naomi Campbell

The only circuit with an overpass, and its own fairground, Suzuka is a favourite with the drivers. The 130 degree 130R left-hander is a flat-out masterpiece, where only the best in the world attempt to overtake. After the race, most of the drivers head to the nearby karaoke cabins to murder rock ballads.

## Brazilian Grand Prix
*Sao Paulo*

Few fans are as passionate as the chanting, samba-drum-wielding Brazilian crowds that cram into the Interlagos track every year. The tarmac is famously bumpy, but the atmosphere is so charged that it's always a highlight of the season. The long run into the downhill first corner is ideal for overtaking.

**Celebrity guest:** Brazilian football legend Pelé

## Abu Dhabi Grand Prix
*Yas Marina Circuit*

This new track is a great unknown for the drivers, but the technology involved promises to make it one of the best. Not only that, the track actually passes through a hotel, which itself changes colour at night. Part of the pit lane is underground, and the circuit runs along the edge of a harbour, like Monaco.

**Celebrity guest:** TBA

# WHERE'S THE VENUE?

1

**2**

# WHERE'S THE VENUE?

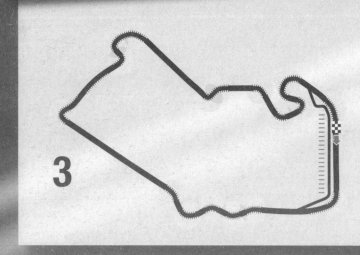

3

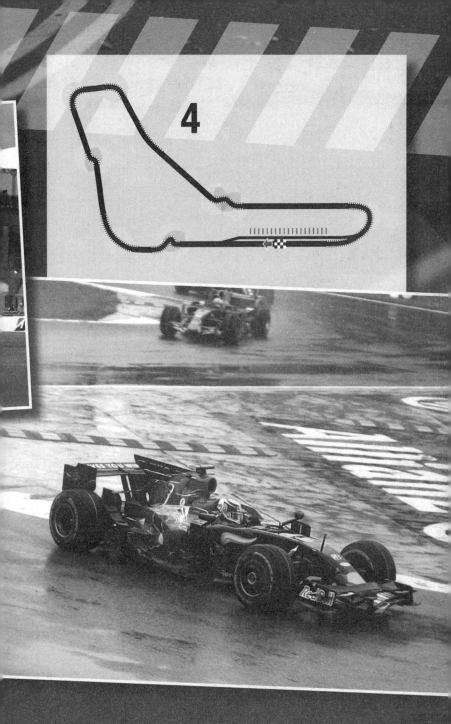

**4**

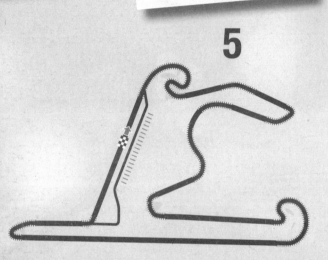

5

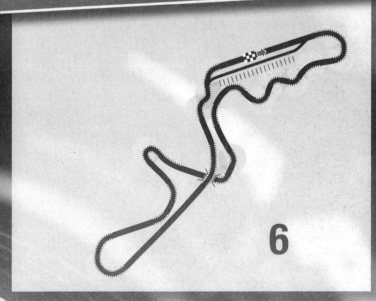

**6**

7

**9**

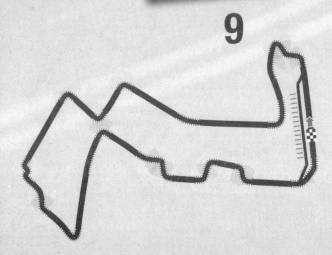

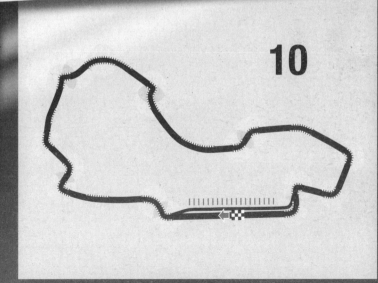

10

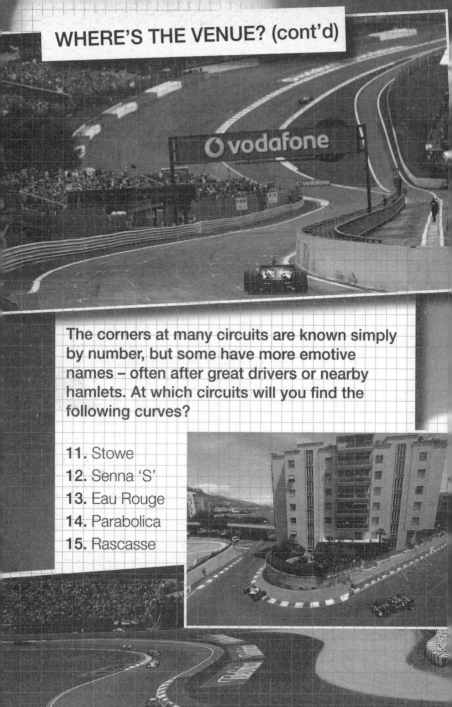

The corners at many circuits are known simply by number, but some have more emotive names – often after great drivers or nearby hamlets. At which circuits will you find the following curves?

**11.** Stowe
**12.** Senna 'S'
**13.** Eau Rouge
**14.** Parabolica
**15.** Rascasse

It's always sad when a Grand Prix track drops off the calendar. In which countries will you find the following former F1 circuits?

**16.** Kyalami
**17.** Zolder
**18.** TI Aida
**19.** A1 Ring
**20.** Montjuich Park

# CHAMPIONS OF THE WORLD

It's one thing to win a race; it's an altogether more Herculean task to win a world championship. Zero mistakes and concrete reliability are every bit as important as speed. Here are 30 men who won the ultimate prize, and one who did it seven times.

# SEVEN

**Michael Schumacher**
(1994, 1995, 2000, 2001, 2002, 2003, 2004)

# FIVE

**Juan Manuel Fangio**
(1951, 1954, 1955, 1956, 1957)

# FOUR

**Alain Prost**
(1985, 1986, 1989, 1993)

Alain Prost

# THREE

**Jack Brabham**
(1959, 1960, 1966)

**Jackie Stewart**
(1969, 1971, 1973)

**Niki Lauda**
(1975, 1977, 1984)

**Nelson Piquet**
(1981, 1983, 1987)

**Ayrton Senna**
(1988, 1990, 1991)

Ayrton Senna

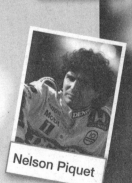
Nelson Piquet

## TWO

**Alberto Ascari** (1952, 1953)

**Graham Hill** (1962, 1968)

**Jim Clark** (1963, 1965)

**Emerson Fittipaldi** (1972, 1974)

**Mika Hakkinen** (1998, 1999)

**Fernando Alonso** (2005, 2006)

Fernando Alonso

## ONE

**Giuseppe Farina** (1950)

**Mike Hawthorn** (1958)

**Phil Hill** (1961)

**John Surtees** (1964)

**Denny Hulme** (1967)

**Jochen Rindt** (1970)

**James Hunt** (1976)

Mika Hakkinen

Michael Schumacher

Michael Schumacher was the dominant driver of his day, winning an unprecedented seven titles. But he had some competition. Which drivers finished second to Michael in the following years?

Mario Andretti

Mario **Andretti** (1978)

Jody **Scheckter** (1979)

Alan **Jones** (1980)

Keke **Rosberg** (1982)

Nigel **Mansell** (1992)

Damon **Hill** (1996)

Jacques **Villeneuve** (1997)

Kimi **Räikkönen** (2007)

Lewis **Hamilton** (2008)

Keke Rosberg

Damon Hill

**1)** 1994
**2)** 1995
**3)** 2000

**4)** 2001
**5)** 2002

**6)** 2003
**7)** 2004

# GUESS WHO IT IS

Look at this face and you're looking at no less than 13 world championships. But who do the mouth and chin, nose, eyes and cap fit?

# FASTEST FIGURES FIRST

Formula One™ racing is always quick. But this is when it was quickest . . .

Highest-ever average speed over a Grand Prix distance: **Michael Schumacher (Ferrari), 2003 Italian Grand Prix – 247.58km/h average speed.**

Highest-ever average speed in a pole position lap: **Juan Pablo Montoya (Williams BMW), 2002 Italian Grand Prix – 259.5km/h average speed**

# Guess the Team

Can you identify the teams in these pictures? Write the team names on the white panels and check your answers at the back of the book on page 97.

**1**

**6**

**7**

**8**

**9**

10

11

**14**

**15**

Closest-ever pole position:
**1st Jacques Villeneuve (Williams-Renault) –**
2nd Michael Schumacher (Ferrari) – 3rd Heinz-Harald Frentzen (Williams-Renault), 1997 European Grand Prix – 0.000 seconds gap.
All three drivers posted a qualifying time of 1:21.072.

Closest-ever Grand Prix finish:
**1st Peter Gethin (B.R.M) –**
**2nd Ronnie Peterson (March),**
1971 Italian Grand Prix – 0.010 seconds.

# TEAMS THAT ARE NO LONGER

Here are some of the many teams that have fallen by the wayside since the World Championship started.

AFM, **AGS,** Alfa Romeo, **Alta,** Amon, **Andrea Moda,** Apollon, **Arrows,** Aston-Butterworth, **Aston-Martin,** ATS, **ATS (different),** BAR, **Bellasi,** Boro, **Brabham**, BRM, **BRP,** Bugatti, **Cisitalia,** Coloni, **Connaught,** Connew, **Cooper,** Dallara, **de Tomaso,** Derrington-Francis, **Eagle,** Emeryson, **EMW,** ENB, **Ensign,** ERA, **Euro Brun,** Ferguson, **Fittipaldi,** Fondmetal, **Footwork,** Forti, **Frazer-Nash,** Fry, **Gilby,** Gordini, **Hesketh,** Hill, **Honda,** HWM, **Jaguar,** JBW, **Jordan,** Kauhsen, **Klenk-Meteor,**

Kojima, **Lamborghini,** Lancia, **Larrousse,** LDS, **Lec,** Leyton House, **Life,** Ligier, **Lola,** Lotus, **Lyncar,** Maki, **March,** Martini, **Maserati,** Matra, **McGuire,** Mercedes, **Merzario,** MF1 Racing, **Milano,** Minardi, **Onyx,** OSCA, **Osella,** Pacific, **Parnelli,** Penske, **Porsche,** Prost, **RAM,** Rebaque, **Rial,** Sauber, **Scarab,** Schroeder, **Scirocco,** Shadow, **Shannon,** Simca-Gordini, **Simtek,** Spirit, **Spyker,** Stebro, **Stewart,** Super Aguri, **Surtees,** Talbot-Lago, **Tec-Mec,** Tecno, **Theodore,** Token, **Toleman,** Trojan, **Tyrrell,** Vanwall, **Veritas,** Wolf, **Zakspeed.**

# WHAT'S IN A NAME?

With so many unpronounceable names in F1™ racing, it's no surprise that nick-names are common. Here are some silly names that managed to stick.

### José Froilán 'The Pampas Bull' González

Also called 'El Cabezon' (Fat Head) by his compatriots, González was large from birth, rather than from eating too many Argentinean steaks. Though Enzo Ferrari wondered how someone who sweated so much could drive so well, The Pampas Bull was very successful, claiming Ferrari's first Grand Prix victory at Silverstone in 1951.

### Niki 'The Rat' Lauda

Thanks to his prominent front teeth, Lauda was nicknamed 'The Mouse'. But as he graduated up through the different formulae, he was promoted to 'Super Mouse', 'Super Rat' and, with a trilogy of F1 racing championships under his belt (not something associated with the average rodent), 'King Rat'. Ultimately, these days, he just goes by 'The Rat'.

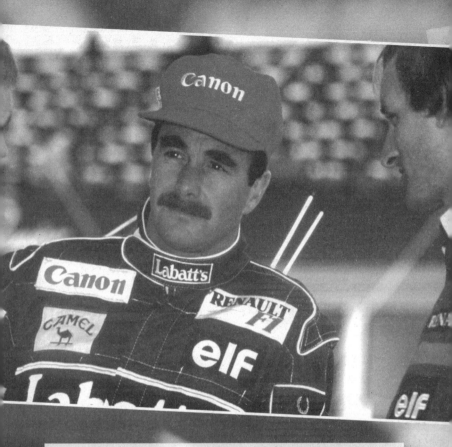

## Nigel 'Il Leone' Mansell

The Italian fans, known as the Tifosi, took Nigel
Mansell to their hearts when he raced for Ferrari,
and they bestowed the title 'The Lion' upon the
Englishman. It was his never-say-die spirit they
admired and, after all, not everyone who narrowly
avoided a broken spine would sneak out of
hospital early, pretending to be on a trip to the
toilet. That, and the fact that his moustache did
have a mane-like quality.

# Denny 'The Bear' Hulme

New Zealander Hulme became known as 'The Bear' due to his strong appearance and sometimes gruff demeanour, although in truth he was very courteous. In fact, his tenure as the head of the Grand Prix Drivers' Association was cut short because he was just too polite. Early on in his career, his habit of driving without shoes earned him the nickname 'The Barefoot Boy'.

# Vittorio 'The Monza Gorilla' Brambilla

Brambilla's ape-related nickname referred to his unrefined, uncompromising driving style, which won him his only Grand Prix victory at the wet Österreichring in 1975. He also enjoyed giving bone-crushing handshakes and, once the unfortunate recipient had turned away, a swift punch to the back of the neck, which he considered a sign of affection.

See if you can identify which drivers are known by these nicknames:

A) The Shunt
B) Swerve
C) The Iceman
D) Kamikaze
E) Hermann the German
F) Quick Nick

# Alain 'The Professor' Prost

Prost's academic nickname came from his studious, considered approach to racing and the high level of technical feedback he gave to his engineers, leading some to speculate who had actually designed the car. Professorships also take many years to acquire, while Prost waited six years before claiming his first of four world titles.

# FLAG IT UP

**1.** CHEQUERED FLAG

**2.** RED FLAG

**3.** YELLOW FLAG

**4.** BLACK FLAG

**5.** YELLOW AND RED STRIPED FLAG

You've got to keep your eyes on the road ahead, on the car behind, and on the instruments on your dashboard. You've got enough on your plate, really, but ignore the marshal's flags at your peril – you could be disqualified. What do these flags mean, and what must you do if they're waved in front of you? **Match the flag to the description.** Get it wrong, and you'll get a thick ear from the stewards, not to mention a huge fine.

**A)** The race has been stopped, this time prematurely.

**B)** A hazard has been cleared and the race is underway again.

**C)** You are about to be lapped and you must allow the car behind you to overtake you.

**D)** Your car has a mechanical problem and you must pit immediately.

**E)** The race has finished.

**F)** You are disqualified. Return to the pits immediately.

**G)** There is a hazard ahead and overtaking is prohibited.

**H)** You're being accused of unsportsmanlike behaviour, and need to take warning.

**I)** There's a slow moving vehicle on the track, such as the safety car.

**J)** There is oil on the track.

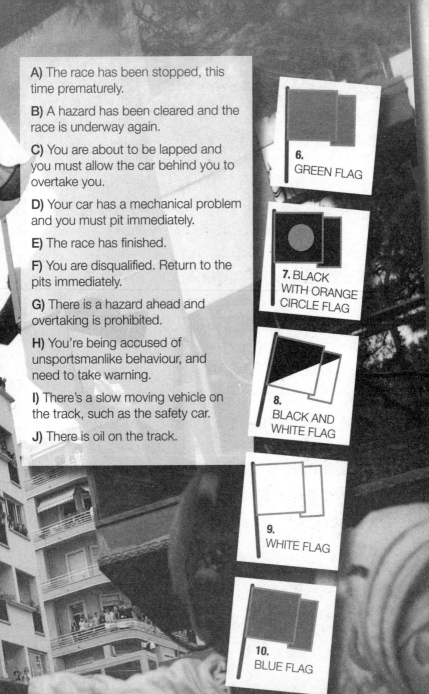

**6.** GREEN FLAG

**7.** BLACK WITH ORANGE CIRCLE FLAG

**8.** BLACK AND WHITE FLAG

**9.** WHITE FLAG

**10.** BLUE FLAG

# PROBABLY THE BEST MOVE OF ALL TIME

### Spa, August 27th 2000, Lap 41

The question that plagues the minds of all racing enthusiasts – what was the greatest overtaking move ever? Was it Jacques Villeneuve going round the outside of Michael Schumacher at Estoril in 1996? Ten points for crazy. Was it Nigel Mansell passing Gerhard Berger the long way round in Mexico in 1990? About as dangerous as it gets! But the ultimate move ever was Mika Hakkinen's audacious pass on Schumi at the 2000 Belgian Grand Prix, using Ricardo Zonta as a springboard. Here's how he did it . . .

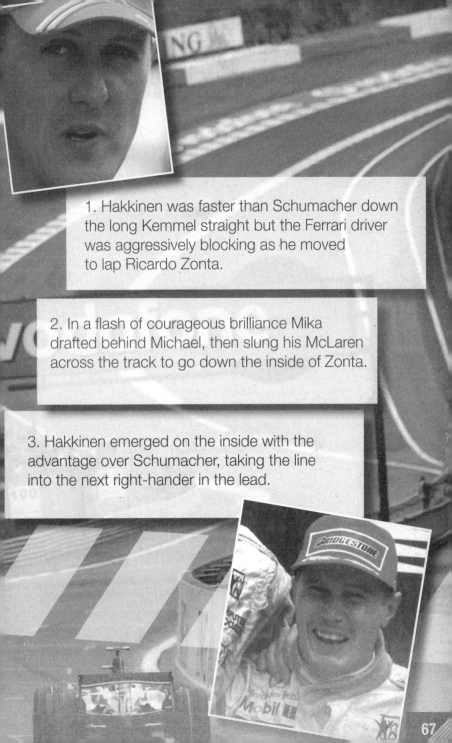

1. Hakkinen was faster than Schumacher down the long Kemmel straight but the Ferrari driver was aggressively blocking as he moved to lap Ricardo Zonta.

2. In a flash of courageous brilliance Mika drafted behind Michael, then slung his McLaren across the track to go down the inside of Zonta.

3. Hakkinen emerged on the inside with the advantage over Schumacher, taking the line into the next right-hander in the lead.

# FEAR FACTOR

Formula One™ drivers are courageous heroes who fear nothing, right? Wrong. They all have an Achilles' heel that will leave them quivering under the bed, unable to come out in time for qualifying. Match the faces opposite to the fears below.

A horse (Equinophobia)

A shark (Selachophobia)

An aeroplane (Aerophobia)

A mouse (Musophobia)

A crowd (Agoraphobia)

The Eiffel Tower (Acrophobia)

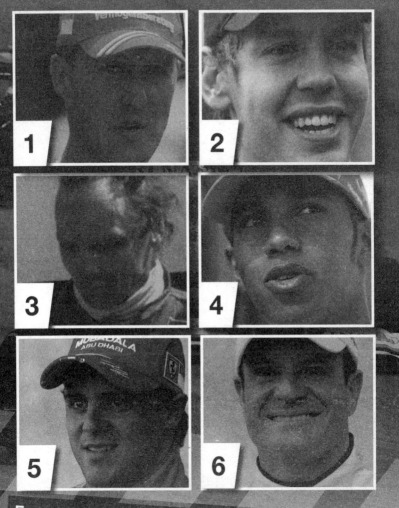

1

2

3

4

5

6

Even action man Mark Webber gets scared occasionally. Well, once. Which of these three activities does 'Webbo' say he would find the scariest?

A) Skydiving

B) Riding a MotoGP bike

C) Cage diving with great white sharks

# HAIRY MOMENTS

Nigel Mansell used to claim that the sight of Union Jacks at Silverstone made him two seconds a lap faster. Imagine the speed his moustache must have given him. Yes, Formula One racing is a hairy sport, where whiskers can make you a winner.

## Bushy beards

Nick Heidfeld may provide the paddock's current bearded wonderment, but it's by no means a new fashion. The king of curly fuzz was an Austrian called Harald Ertl who failed to score a single championship point from his 28 Grands Prix but outscored all the greats with a beard as bushy as a privet hedge and a moustache that was simply preposterous. Ertl was a journalist who managed to attract enough sponsorship to compete with Hesketh, Ensign and ATS as an enthusiastic amateur. The amiable Ertl was also one of the four drivers who helped pull Niki Lauda from his burning Ferrari in 1976.

## Manly moustaches

While Nigel Mansell's moustache undermined his status as a speed demon, making him look more like a geography teacher, the

man who really made it work was Graham Hill. As British as a tweed jacket with leather elbow patches and rain, Damon's dad managed to win the world championship twice, Monaco five times, and both Le Mans and the Indy 500, making him a true giant of motorsport. But he's best remembered for a dashing 'tash that was so sharp you could cut yourself on it.

## Shocking sideburns

For sideburns we have Jackie Stewart and Emerson Fittipaldi. These men were pioneers of the 1970s 'pork chop' movement, and 'Emo' still wears his to this day. They took him to two world championships and the knighted Sir Jackie to three.

**Which of these F1 racing pilots has never given up the use of a razor?**

Gerhard Berger    Jacques Villeneuve
John Watson    Jenson Button

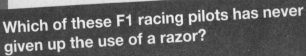

# Menu de Jour

Petroleum companies spend many millions of pounds developing the ultimate performance fuels. For the driver, food is fuel, and what he eats is of paramount importance.

But it wasn't always this way. Until the modern era dawned, if a driver was hungry he ate whatever was nearby. Quite literally, in Tazio Nuvolari's case. The great 1930s racer once smashed through a butcher's shop window when racing in the Targa Florio. He then attempted to return the car to the road, but not before he helped himself to a ham.

Jim Clark's favourite pre-race meal was steak and chips, while Gilles Villeneuve loved hamburgers, fries and milkshakes. The driver who kick-started the healthy eating initiative was Niki Lauda who, when recovering from a crash in 1976, hired a fitness guru and started to eat nutritionally balanced meals. Drivers would never look at a plate of chips again . . .

Here are some typical driver meals, back in 1969 and today:

# 1969

Breakfast
**Bacon, eggs, baked beans, toast**

■■■■■

Mid-morning snack
**Coffee, biscuits**

■■■■■

Lunch
**Minestrone soup**
**Macaroni cheese**
**Veal cutlet in breadcrumbs**
**Apple tart**
**Coffee, chocolates**

■■■■■

Mid-afternoon snack
**Chocolate bar**

■■■■■

Dinner
**Spaghetti bolognese**
**Roast beef in a red**
**wine sauce**
**Chocolate cake**

# 2009

Breakfast
**Cereal (no milk) and fruit**

■■■■■

Mid-morning snack
**Fruit and a handful of nuts**

■■■■■

Lunch
**Pasta with fresh**
**tomato sauce**

■■■■■

Mid-afternoon snack
**Cereal (no milk)**
**and fruit**

■■■■■

Dinner
**Steamed fish**
**and spinach**

# HAVE YOU GOT WHAT IT TAKES?

OK, you have a talent behind the wheel. But there's more to F1™ racing than driving, you know . . . Sheer speed isn't enough. There are difficult decisions to be made on the road to championship glory. Put yourself in the situations on pages 75-77 and choose from the four options. There are right answers, wrong answers and sometimes in-between answers, and plenty of points up for grabs – 40 beautiful, shiny world championship points. Fail to answer, and it's the black flag for you . . .

**1.** Well done, you're an F1 driver and have been paid your first month's enormous wages. Where do you go house hunting?

**A)** Monaco
**B)** Switzerland
**C)** Close to the factory
**D)** Other

**2.** You have a choice of teammate. Do you opt for . . .

**A)** Your old friend and teammate from GP2 with whom you came up through the ranks and who you've known since you were in karts, aged eight.
**B)** The son of a former Grand Prix driver, who you regularly beat in Formula Renault.
**C)** That Japanese kid who crashed everything in the Formula 3 Euro Series.
**D)** A random Brazilian.

**3.** Your dad has been the guiding hand behind your path to F1 racing. But it's the big time now and everyone says you need a 'proper' manager. Do you . . .

**A)** Ignore what they say and keep him on.
**B)** Get Michael Schumacher's old manager.
**C)** Bring him to the races and tell him to have fun, as long as he keeps his mouth shut.
**D)** Decide that being forced to choose between career and family is too high a price to pay for success, and quit.

**4. At a press conference, a journalist from Sprockets Gazette asks you to name your favourite driver of all time. Who do you name?**
A) Alain Prost
B) Ayrton Senna
C) Your dad
D) Michael Schumacher

**5. Your website editor needs more 'lifestyle content'. But while this might prelude a gross invasion of your privacy, all he wants to know is what music you listen to. So, what's on your iPod?**
A) U2
B) Amy Winehouse
C) Kid Rock
D) Ethiopian jazz legend Mulatu Astatke

**6. The team gives you its latest dull hybrid people carrier to drive. How do you respond?**

**A)** "It's the 21st century and we've all got to do our bit for the environment."

**B)** "Great, no need to bother with hotels. I can fold down the seats and camp in the back."

**C)** Put it on eBay.

**D)** Take it out and deliberately ruin it.

**7. Time to renegotiate your contract. The car manufacturer's president takes you and your manager out for lunch. What do you order?**

**A)** Pasta and green salad.

**B)** Sushi and tempura.

**C)** Burger and fries.

**D)** Filet mignon and fine wines.

**8. You're bored in the off-season, as you wait for the start of a new campaign. Do you . . .**

**A)** Rent a Swiss chalet for three months, train furiously, drink only water, eat only nutritionally perfect meals and emerge from the hills ready to take on the world.

**B)** Rent a gorilla suit and enter a snowmobile race under the name 'James Hunt'.

**C)** Read philosophy books in order to understand racecar driving as an existential construct.

**D)** Set up a teepee outside the McLaren Technology Centre and send smoke-signals everyday, indicating to the team principal that he doesn't know what he's missing.

# WINNING MOVES

A raised fist, a little jump, a wave to the crowd: podium celebrations are a little predictable. What you need is a proper victory dance, to stand out from the crowd. Here's how to make your podium party perfect . . .

## 1. The Klinsmann

German football legend Jürgen Klinsmann patented this full-length celebration dive after scoring a goal. A wet-race followed by a slippery podium makes this a must-do for any driver.

## 2. The balancing act

Delight your fans with this demanding yet show-stopping piece of bottle-balancing chin action.

### 3. The Caterpillar

Only for the truly
committed risk takers,
but F1 drivers are
supposed to be the
ultimate adventurers.
Break-dance your way
to immortality.

### 4. The zen master

Victory is short lived, true fulfilment can only
be found through meditation and
thrashing your teammate every other
weekend. Levitation will complete
your god-like image.

# SENNAPHORE

Semaphore is a messaging device originally used by sailors thousands of years ago to communicate with each other. F1™ teams use pit boards and sophisticated radios to do the same thing. But here we have **'Sennaphore'**. Study the guide to semaphore and try to work out what Ayrton Senna wants to say…

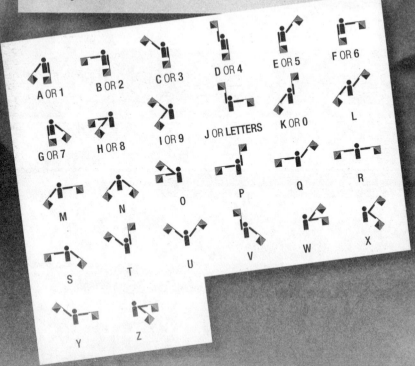

## 1. Who was Ayrton's greatest rival?

## 2. What was Ayrton's favourite track?

## 3. What was Ayrton's favourite hobby?

## 4. What star sign was Ayrton?

## 5. Which was Ayrton's first F1 racing team?

# MULTIPLE CHOICE
## QUESTIONNAIRE

**1.** You've scored third place in the Bahrain Grand Prix. Well done. Help yourself to a drink on the podium. But what is it that you're offered?

**A)** Non-alcoholic sparkling fruit juice
**B)** Sparkling water
**C)** Full-fat milk
**D)** Champagne

**2.** For which team did Mika Hakkinen drive before he joined McLaren in 1993?

**A)** Williams
**B)** Arrows
**C)** Sauber
**D)** Lotus

**3.** Monaco's Louis Chiron became the oldest driver to ever compete in a Grand Prix in 1955. But how old was he?

**A)** 47
**B)** 50
**C)** 53
**D)** 55

**4.** Many F1 drivers aren't old enough to rent a car. Who was the youngest driver to ever compete in a Grand Prix?

**A)** Sebastian Vettel
**B)** Lewis Hamilton
**C)** Mike Thackwell
**D)** Esteban Tuero

**5.** Which driver has scored the most pole positions in history?

**A)** Ayrton Senna
**B)** Michael Schumacher
**C)** Jim Clark
**D)** Alain Prost

**6.** Back in the day, the Indianapolis 500 counted as a round of the F1 world championship. Which of these F1 world champions has not won the famous Indy 500?

**A)** Graham Hill
**B)** Mario Andretti
**C)** Nigel Mansell
**D)** Jacques Villeneuve

**7.** Monaco is the toughest test of driver precision. Who won the most ever Monaco Grands Prix?

**A)** Graham Hill
**B)** Michael Schumacher
**C)** Ayrton Senna
**D)** David Coulthard

**8.** In 1995, on which circuit did Michael Schumacher win from sixteenth on the grid?

**A)** Hockenheim
**B)** Silverstone
**C)** Nürburgring
**D)** Spa-Francorchamps

**9.** At the rain-soaked 2003 Brazilian Grand

Prix, the stewards incorrectly handed victory to Kimi Räikkönen. The real winner was crowned a week later. Who was victory ultimately handed to?

**A)** Cristiano da Matta
**B)** Mark Webber
**C)** Fernando Alonso
**D)** Giancarlo Fisichella

**10.** There have been a few female drivers in F1 racing. Who is the only female driver to have scored a point?

**A)** Desire Wilson
**B)** Lella Lombardi
**C)** Giovanna Amati
**D)** Danica Patrick

**11.** Which countries hosted F1 races at four different venues from 1950 onwards (excluding North America)?

**A)** Belgium and Brazil
**B)** Japan and Spain
**C)** Britain and France
**D)** Germany and Italy

**12.** Why was the 1996 Monaco Grand Prix slightly bizarre for David Coulthard?

**A)** He raced with three wheels.
**B)** He was wearing Michael Schumacher's helmet.
**C)** He had two broken ribs.
**D)** He wasn't wearing trousers.

**13.** There have been more world champions from Britain than any other country. But which of these drivers has not yet been knighted by the Queen?

**A)** Stirling Moss
**B)** Jack Brabham
**C)** Damon Hill
**D)** Jackie Stewart

**14.** Which driver gave Benetton their first F1 race win in 1986 and ironically their last ever win in 1997?

**A)** Teo Fabi
**B)** Jean Alesi
**C)** Gerhard Berger
**D)** Riccardo Patrese

**15.** The Tyrrell team launched a very odd car in 1976. What was so odd about it?

**A)** It had six wheels.
**B)** It had two cockpits.
**C)** It was powered by a fan.
**D)** It was the first car to use a turbo engine.

**16.** Formula One racing was a bit predictable in 1988. Which team won 15 out of 16 races?

**A)** McLaren
**B)** Ferrari
**C)** Williams
**D)** Lotus

**17.** McLarens, these days, are silver. But that wasn't always the case. What colour was the first

**McLaren Formula One car?**

**A)** White
**B)** Black
**C)** Green
**D)** Orange

**18.** **Which of these drivers did not make his Formula One debut in a Minardi?**

**A)** Mark Webber
**B)** Jarno Trulli
**C)** Fernando Alonso
**D)** Kimi Räikkönen

**19.** Which of these drivers did not make his Formula One racing debut in a Sauber?

A) Heinz-Harald Frentzen
B) Felipe Massa
C) Kimi Räikkönen
D) Nick Heidfeld

**20.** Which of these drivers did not make his Formula One racing debut in a Jordan?

A) Michael Schumacher
B) Ralf Schumacher
C) Timo Glock
D) Sébastien Bourdais

**21.** James Hunt wasn't just a world-champion racing-driver. In what other competition did he win a championship?

A) Snooker
B) Chess
C) Cricket
D) Budgerigar breeding

## 22. What was Nigel Mansell's part-time job?

**A)** Accountant
**B)** Special police constable
**C)** Actor
**D)** Taxi driver

## 23. Many countries would like their own race. Which of these countries has not yet hosted a Grand Prix?

**A)** Argentina
**B)** India
**C)** Netherlands
**D)** South Africa

**Here are some anagrams – words made up from the letters of famous names.**

**Can you identify the following three F1 racing personalities?**

**24.** Claim much cash here

**25.** Failing his local race

**26.** Recent obscene lie

The following photographs are all of British drivers. Can you identify them?

27.

28.

29.

30.

# THE *ULTIMATE* F1™ RACING QUIZ

This is the one you've been gearing up for! Do you think you can pass the ultimate tricky quiz with flying colours?

**1. In which country is a Grand Prix held at night?**

**2. Who is the youngest driver ever to win a Grand Prix?**

**3. Who is the youngest driver ever to win a world championship?**

**4. Which driver has made the most Grand Prix starts ever?**

**5. The 'Tifosi' are renowned for their love of F1 racing and one team in particular. Which team?**

**6. Lewis Hamilton's girlfriend, Nicole Scherzinger, is a singer in which pop band?**

**7. Which is the only existing team to have been in F1 racing since the world championship started in 1950?**

**8. In 1984, which British driver famously blamed a painted white line for causing his suspension**

damage and retirement from the lead of the Monaco Grand Prix?

9. Which decade saw four British drivers claim six F1 drivers' titles?

10. Which British driver made his F1 racing debut with Williams BMW in 2000?

11. At which circuit did Michael Schumacher break his leg in 1999?

12. Who is the only driver to have been world champion on two wheels as well as four?

13. In which country will you find the famous Interlagos circuit?

14. What English town was Lewis Hamilton born in?

15. What nationality was the Super Aguri team?

16. Who was the last Frenchman to win a Grand Prix, and which one was it?

17. Who was the first British world champion?

18. What was the name of director John Frankenheimer's 1966 racing movie?

19. There are a series of 'Michael Schumacher' skyscrapers being built around the world. Seven in total, to celebrate his seven titles. Where has the first one been built?

20. Which F1 racing world champion owns a commercial airline?

21. What links Luciano Burti, Marc Gene and Luca Badoer?

22. On what TV show did Lewis Hamilton make his first ever appearance?

23. What was David Coulthard's best championship result, and in what year?

24. How many F1 world champions has Finland produced, and can you name them?

25. Ayrton Senna was on course to win the 1988 Italian Grand Prix, but he hit Williams' Jean-Louis Schlesser and that was the end of his race. The crowd went wild. Who won, and for which team?

26. At what circuit would you find the 'Casino Square' section?

27. Woking, Surrey, is the home of which F1 racing team?

28. Which current F1 racing circuit is the fastest?

29. In what year did Lewis Hamilton make his debut, and at which race?

30. What football club does Renault team principal Flavio Briatore co-own?

31. What is the name of Formula One racing's governing body?

32. Which circuit currently hosts the European Grand Prix?

33. How were Brazilian F1 drivers Emerson Fittipaldi and Wilson Fittipaldi related?

34. Kimi Räikkönen crashed into which driver at the 2008 Monaco Grand Prix?

35. Alex Zanardi first drove for the Lotus team. What was the last F1 team he drove for?

36. In what series did Nigel Mansell race, and win the championship, in 1993?

37. What was strange about the 1982 South African Grand Prix?

38. Who is currently the highest paid driver in Formula One racing?

39. The very first Grand Prix was held in 1906 in France, at Le Mans. It was won by a Hungarian called Ferenc Szisz. What make of car was he driving?

40. Who won the first ever world championship Grand Prix, at Silverstone, in 1950?

# ANSWERS

## Pages 12-15
### THE DRIVERS

1) Nico Rosberg
2) Adrian Sutil
3) Robert Kubica
4) Jenson Button
5) Kazuki Nakajima
6) Timo Glock
7) Jarno Trulli
8) Sebastian Vettel
9) Felipe Massa
10) Sébastien Bourdais
11) Heikki Kovalainen
12) Fernando Alonso
13) Sébastien Buemi
14) Giancarlo Fisichella
15) Rubens Barrichello
16) Kimi Räikkönen
17) Nick Heidfeld
18) Mark Webber
19) Lewis Hamilton
20) Nelson Piquet Jr

## Pages 16-17
### WHO'S LID IS IT ANYWAY?

A) Robert Kubica
B) Lewis Hamilton
C) Kazuki Nakajima
D) Sébastian Bourdais
E) Timo Glock
F) Nick Heidfeld
G) Rubens Barrichello
H) Adrian Sutil
I) Felipe Massa
J) Nelson Piquet Jr
K) Sébastien Buemi
L) Jenson Button
M) Heikki Kovalainen
N) Nico Rosberg
O) Giancarlo Fisichella
P) Fernando Alonso
Q) Sebastian Vettel
R) Mark Webber
S) Kimi Räikkönen
T) Jarno Trulli

## Pages 22-23
### LOGO LOWDOWN

A) Brawn GP
B) Red Bull Racing
C) Williams
D) Ferrari
E) Renault
F) McLaren
G) Scuderia Toro Rosso
H) BMW Sauber
I) Force India
J) Toyota

## Pages 30-41
### WHERE'S THE VENUE?

1) Hungaroring
2) Monaco
3) Silverstone
4) Monza
5) Shanghai
6) Suzuka
7) Turkey
8) Malaysia
9) Singapore
10) Melbourne
11) Silverstone
12) Interlagos

13) Spa-Francorchamps
14) Monza
15) Monaco
16) South Africa
17) Belgium
18) Japan
19) Austria
20) Spain

7 = Renault
8 = Toyota
9 = Brawn GP
10 = Williams
11 = Brawn GP
12 = BMW Sauber
13 = McLaren
14 = Brawn GP
15 = Williams

*Page 45*
## CHAMPIONS OF THE WORLD
1) 1994 – Damon Hill
2) 1995 – Damon Hill
3) 2000 – Mika Hakkinen
4) 2001 – David Coulthard
5) 2002 – Rubens Barrichello
6) 2003 – Kimi Räikkönen
7) 2004 – Rubens Barrichello

*Pages 46-47*
## GUESS WHO IT IS
**Cap:** Ayrton Senna
**Eyes:** Nelson Piquet
**Nose:** Ayrton Senna
**Mouth and chin:** Michael Schumacher

*Pages 49-56*
## GUESS THE TEAM
1 = Force India
2 = Ferrari
3 = Toro Rosso
4 = Renault
5 = Red Bull Racing
6 = BMW Sauber

*Page 62*
## WHAT'S IN A NAME?
**A) The Shunt:** James Hunt
**B) Swerve:** Eddie Irvine
**C) The Iceman:** Kimi Räikkönen
**D) Kamikaze:** Ukyo Katayama
**E) Hermann the German:** Jochen Mass
**F) Quick Nick:** Nick Heidfeld

*Pages 64-65*
## FLAG IT UP
1 = E
2 = A
3 = G
4 = F
5 = J
6 = B
7 = D
8 = H
9 = I
10 = C

*Pages 68-69*
**FEAR FACTOR**

**1) Michael Schumacher =** Agoraphobia. Michael finds large crowds of people alarming, often preventing him from attending big football matches.

**2) Sebastian Vettel =** Musophobia. Seb is afraid of mice. They make him feel sick.

**3) Niki Lauda =** Equinophobia. Lauda is scared of horses, due to the time he got stuck in the middle of a frenzied group of fans on horseback after winning the 1975 Italian Grand Prix.

**4) Lewis Hamilton =** Selachophobia. Lewis' worst nightmare takes the form of great white sharks.

**5) Felipe Massa =** Acrophobia. Felipe may someday scale the heights of F1 racing, but high altitude is a problem for the Brazilian.

**6) Rubens Barrichello =** Aerophobia. Rubens has travelled over three million miles by aeroplane, so you would have thought he'd be used to it. But he's no fan of flying.

A - Skydiving

*Page 71*
**HAIRY MOMENTS**
Gerhard Berger

*Pages 74-77*
**HAVE YOU GOT WHAT IT TAKES?**
**1) 'B' plus 'D'**
**If you chose 'B' with 'D' you earn the full 5 points:** How can you expect to store all your trophies in one house?
**If you chose 'B' score 4 points:** You've found your

rightful place among your peers, just at the bottom of Fernando's garden.

**If you chose 'A' score 1 point:** You're being too 90s. The only drivers you'll meet in Monaco will be your dad's age, or the sons of drivers your dad's age.

**If you scored 'C' then you score 0:** You're trapped in your F3 mindset, snap out of it. You're only allowed to live near the factory if your team is BMW Sauber.

**If you chose 'D' on its own you get zero points:** You've sold your soul to F1 racing. You can't live just anywhere, you know . . .

## 2) 'A'

**If you chose 'A' you score 5 points:** You would only be friends with your former GP2 teammate if you were considerably quicker than him.

**If you chose 'B', 'C' or 'D' you score 0 points:** 'B' is the son of a former driver, probably so well connected that the son could finish a race the Tuesday after the start and he still wouldn't be fired. 'C' is Japanese and comes with so much sponsorship and/or free engines that you can't ever compete. 'D' might be erratic but South Americans are usually far too quick.

## 3) 'B'

**If you chose 'B' you score 5 points:** Look what he did for Michael Schumacher. And for Ralf Schumacher – and if he could get Ralf a $16 million-a-year contract, you'll be a billionaire by 30.

**If you chose 'C' you score 3 points:** The so-called Jenson Button approach is business-effective, benign to your family relations and media-friendly.

**If you chose 'A' you score 1 point:** You've proved you're a human being and therefore deserve some small reward.

**If you chose 'D' you score 0 points:** You may well be a loser all your life.

## 4) 'D'

**If you chose 'D' you score 5 points:** It says super-fit,

super-fast, superman. It also says I'm very young, extremely ambitious, and prepared to run over my own grandmother to get to the very top. F1 racing gold.

**If you chose 'A' you score 4 points:** Good if you're going to a team run by a studious engineer who values accurate feedback, consistent laptimes and clean living.

**If you chose 'C' you score 3 points:** Sweet, and useful if you want to drive for Williams.

**If you chose 'B' you score 2 points:** You had better be certain this team wants an emotional uber-talent who won't hesitate to tell the team what they're doing wrong, or punch a back-marker if he doesn't get out of the way. Incompatible with the Prost.

## 5) 'A'

**If you chose 'A' you score 5 points:** Nobody ever went wrong listening to U2.

**If you chose 'B' you score 4 points:** A bit risky but good – hint of the bad boy image while remaining basically non-threatening and media friendly.

**If you chose 'C' you score 0 points:** Country-influenced rap music has only one place, and that's NASCAR.

**If you chose 'D' you score 0 points:** F1 racing has no time for intellectuals, get thee back to racing.

## 6) 'D'

**If you chose 'D' you score 5 points:** Fiat van sales went up 37 percent once Michael Schumacher started driving them, so imagine what Michael Schumacher crashing one did for the brand. Besides, the publicity will do wonders for your wild man of F1 racing reputation.

**If you chose 'C' you score 4 points:** If your name is on the registration document, you can probably sell it to a fan for more than the sticker price.

**If you chose 'B' you score 3 points:** In these economically concerning times, your team's cost-cutting efforts might not afford you a hotel anyway.

**If you chose 'A' you score 0 points:** You're in Formula One racing. You fly around the world and race cars. The only meaning of 'green' you know is 'go'.

**7) 'A'**

**If you chose 'A' you score 5 points:** You're an F1 driver. See you at the track first thing tomorrow.

**If you chose 'B' you score 3 points:** Choosing Japanese food will go down well if your team is Japanese. Then again, this lunch might be to break the news to you that your team is pulling out of F1 racing.

**If you chose 'C' you score 0 points:** You are Juan Pablo Montoya, please go to America and hand over that cream cake.

**If you chose 'D' you score 0 points:** You retired from racing 25 years ago, monsieur.

**8) 'B'**

**If you chose 'B' you score 5 points:** If it works for Kimi Räikkönen, who are you to argue?

**If you chose 'A' you score 4 points:** A suitable reward for your dedication and application. But remember, nobody loves a robot, no matter how successful they are.

**If you chose 'D' you score 3 points:** It worked for Lewis Hamilton, after all.

**If you chose 'C' you score 0 points:** Again, the intelligentsia have no place in Formula One racing. Go back to school.

*Pages 80-81*
## SENNAPHORE

**1)** Prost
**2)** Monaco
**3)** Jetski
**4)** Aries
**5)** Toleman

*Pages 82-89*
## MULTIPLE CHOICE QUESTIONNAIRE

**1)** A
**2)** D
**3)** D
**4)** C (19 years, 182 days)

**5)** B
**6)** C
**7)** C (six times)
**8)** D
**9)** D
**10)** B
**11)** C
**12)** B
**13)** C
**14)** C
**15)** A
**16)** A
**17)** D
**18)** D (His debut was with Sauber)
**19)** D (His debut was with Prost)
**20)** D (His debut was with Toro Rosso)
**21)** D
**22)** B
**23)** B
**24)** Michael Schumacher
**25)** Giancarlo Fisichella
**26)** Bernie Ecclestone
**27)** Jenson Button
**28)** Nigel Mansell
**29)** David Coulthard
**30)** Damon Hill

*Pages 90-95*
**THE ULTIMATE F1 RACING QUIZ**

**1)** Singapore
**2)** Sebastian Vettel (21 years, 73 days)
**3)** Lewis Hamilton (23 years, 300 days)
**4)** Rubens Barrichello (correct as of July 2009)
**5)** Ferrari
**6)** Pussycat Dolls
**7)** Ferrari
**8)** Nigel Mansell
**9)** 1960s

10) Jenson Button
11) Silverstone
12) John Surtees
13) Brazil
14) Stevenage
15) Japanese
16) Olivier Panis, 1996 Monaco Grand Prix
17) Mike Hawthorn
18) Grand Prix
19) Dubai, UAE
20) Niki Lauda
21) They're all former F1 drivers that have gone on to test drive for Ferrari
22) The BBC's Blue Peter
23) Second in 2001
24) Three – Keke Rosberg, Mika Hakkinen, Kimi Räikkönen
25) Gerhard Berger, for Ferrari
26) Monaco
27) McLaren
28) Monza
29) 2007 Australian Grand Prix
30) Queens Park Rangers
31) Fédération International de l'Automobile (FIA)
32) Valencia
33) Brothers
34) Adrian Sutil
35) Williams
36) Indy Car
37) The drivers were on strike for part of the race weekend
38) Kimi Räikkönen (estimated at approx £24 million per season)
39) Renault
40) Giuseppe Farina